ISBN 0-85079-131-6

The GAMBOLS

BOOK Nº 32

©1983 Dobs + Barry Appleby

£1.20

"SPECIAL OFFERS" PLEASE GAYE ALTHOUGH SHE KNOWS THEY ARE A TRAP TO LURE HER INTO BUYING THINGS SHE DOESN'T NEED

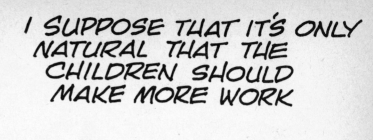

I SUPPOSE THAT IT'S ONLY NATURAL THAT THE CHILDREN SHOULD MAKE MORE WORK

IT IS QUITE SURPRISING HOW MANY PEOPLE NOT ONLY DO NOT SMOKE BUT ALSO OBJECT TO OTHER PEOPLE SMOKING

2576

GEORGE DEAR...

EEK!

I DO WISH YOU WOULDN'T CREEP ABOUT THE HOUSE IN THOSE SOFT SHOES

©1982 Dobs + Barry Appleby

2481

SO NOW WE KNOW WHY WEEK-END BREAKS ARE CHEAPER OUT OF SEASON

©1982 Dobs + Barry Appleby

2482

WE WERE OF COURSE DELIGHTED TO TAKE DELIVERY OF OUR NEW CAR BUT NEVERTHELESS WE FELT VERY SAD TO SEE THE OLD ONE GO

© 1982 Dobs + Barry Appleby

2445

SHE'S LATE HOME

IT'S THE FIRST TIME GAYE'S BEEN OUT IN OUR NEW CAR ON HER OWN

AT LAST

CLUNK

DON'T WORRY DEAR— I HAVEN'T SCRATCHED IT

©1982 Dobs + Barry Appleby

2451

OH NO!

I DON'T CARE IF IT IS COLD IN THE GARAGE

YOU ARE **NOT** BRINGING IT IN HERE EVERY NIGHT

©1982 Dobs + Barry Appleby

2450

GEORGE HATES
HAVING HIS HAIR
CUT AND IT TAKES
A LOT OF NAGGING
FROM GAYE TO
MAKE HIM VISIT
THE BARBER

2472

2357

2359

THE NEXT TIME WE GO OUT TO A RESTAURANT FOR DINNER......

...WE'LL MAKE **SURE** THAT WE **BOTH** CHOOSE GARLIC

© 1982 Dobs + Barry Appleby

2420

I WON'T BE HOME UNTIL LATE THIS EVENING SO WHAT WOULD YOU LIKE ME TO LEAVE YOU FOR YOUR SUPPER?

STATIO

CITY TRAINS

OH - DON'T GO TO ANY TROUBLE

LATER

ME AND MY BIG MOUTH

SARDINES

ALE

© 1982 Dobs + Barry Appleby

2485

GEORGE TAKES AS HIS MOTTO FOR GARDENING THE SAYING OF A FAMOUS MAN WHICH WAS "NEVER HAVE A GARDEN LARGER THAN YOUR WIFE CAN MANAGE ON HER OWN"

FINISHED?

YES

WELL, NOW ADMIT IT — IT WASN'T ANY HARDER THAN WASHING THE CAR, WAS IT?

© 1982 Dobs + Barry Appleby   2362

LET ME KNOW IF I'M IN THE WAY DEAR

© 1982 Dobs + Barry Applebe.

2422

I SEE GEORGE IS AT HOME TO-DAY

YES

HE DECIDED TO TAKE A DAY OFF...

....AND HELP ME WITH THE GARDENING

© 1982 Dobs + Barry Applebe

2363

GAYE HAS A LOT OF DIFFICULTY IN FINDING SHOES THAT FIT REALLY COMFORTABLY

NOW WE COME TO A SELECTION OF
OUR BIGGER CARTOONS WHICH YOU
MAY NOT HAVE SEEN BEFORE

805

807

808

NOW TO WAIT FOR THE SUMP TO EMPTY

OIL

IDEA

BAR

I THOUGHT YOU WERE GOING TO CHANGE THE OIL IN THE CAR

I HAVE

WELL, IT'S THE FUNNIEST SMELLING OIL I'VE EVER KNOWN

809

© 1976 Bob & Barry Appleby

810

GEORGE! YOU'RE GETTING UP—NOT GOING TO BED

812

813

816

817

822

827

829

830

THE NICEST THING ABOUT HOLIDAYS
IN THE SUN IS THE HAPPY MEMORIES
DURING THE DARK COLD NIGHTS

GEORGE NEVER MINDS
HELPING WITH OPINION
POLLS — ESPECIALLY
IF THE QUESTIONS
ARE PUT BY THE RIGHT
INTERVIEWER

PHEW!

SO THE CHILDREN HAVE COME TO VISIT US AGAIN

THOMP THOMP THOMP THOMP

THOMP THOMP THOMP

©1983 Bob's + Barry Appleby

2577

COOEE!— I'M HOME

GEORGE! WHAT.....?

I KNOW WE SAID THAT I WAS NOT TO LET THEM STAY UP LATE..... ..AND I DIDN'T

THEY WENT UP TO BED TWO HOURS AGO

©1983 Bob's + Barry Appleby

2582

FLIVVER!

STOP THROWING ME PEANUTS

© 1983
Dobs +
Barry Appleby

2584

STAY THERE AND WE'LL BRING YOU YOUR MORNING TEA

RIGHT—YOU CARRY IT UP

© 1983
Dobs + Barry Appleby

AND I'LL FOLLOW

2585

IT TAKES GAYE A LONG TIME TO CHOOSE A BOOK IN THE PUBLIC LIBRARY — LONGER TO READ IT AND LONGER STILL TO RETURN IT

HUP!

I WISH THAT WE'D NEVER TAKEN THEM TO THAT CIRCUS

CHOX BIXS

© 1983
Bob's +
Barry Appleby

2586

THE NERVE OF THAT WOMAN

I OFFERED TO STAY AND HELP HER WITH THE WASHING UP

SHE ACTUALLY LET ME

© 1983 Bob's + Barry Appleby

2553

HAVE YOU NOTICED THAT WHEN MOST WOMEN GET A COLD THEY JUST IGNORE IT AND HAVE TO CARRY ON REGARDLESS

DO YOU REMEMBER HOW CHRISTMAS
JUST WENT ON AND ON — IT
NEVER SEEMED TO END

IT'S TIME FOR US TO GO—SO
'BYE FOR NOW UNTIL TOMORROW
MORNING—SEE YOU THEN

©1983 Dobs + Barry Appleby

Published by Express Newspapers Limited, Fleet Street, London, EC4P 4JT, and printed by Purnell and Sons (Book Production) Ltd., Paulton, Bristol.